Land Your Dream Remote Job: The Ultimate Guide to Digital Nomad Careers

By: *El Proen*

Land Your Dream Remote Job: The Ultimate Guide to Digital Nomad Careers

By El Proen

Land Your Dream Remote Job: The Ultimate Guide to Digital Nomad Careers

bout the Author

l Proen is an engineer by profession with a long and successful career in human esources. This unique blend of technical expertise and people management skills has llowed him to excel in building and optimizing remote teams. However, El Proen's assion extends beyond the boardroom. He's a lifelong athlete with a diverse background 1 sports, from the competitive spirit of baseball to the focused discipline of martial arts. his love for physical activity fuels his belief in maintaining a healthy and balanced festyle, a core principle he advocates for in the digital nomad world.

El Proen isn't just an expert on remote work; he's also an e-commerce enthusiast with a een eye for spotting valuable resources and tools. Whether you're navigating the vast narketplace of Amazon or exploring niche platforms like Bonanza, El Proen leverages his xperience to identify the best options for digital nomads seeking to streamline their emote work lifestyle. His passion for remote work, his diverse skillset, and his ommitment to a healthy lifestyle make him the ideal guide for your digital nomad journey. Vith his insights and practical advice, you'll be well-equipped to navigate the exciting world f remote work and create a life filled with freedom, exploration, and fulfillment.

By El Proen

Land Your Dream Remote Job: The Ultimate Guide to Digital Nomad Careers

This book is dedicated to the people who have fueled my fire and supported my dreams, even when they seemed like distant horizons.

To my parents, who instilled in me the value of hard work and the courage to chase adventure. Your unwavering belief in me has been my guiding light.

To my amazing wife, my partner in crime and the sunshine in my life. Your constant love and understanding have given me the freedom to explore and the strength to keep going.

To my incredible sister, my confidante and my biggest cheerleader. Your laughter and support have been a source of endless joy and motivation.

To my precious children, who remind me of the magic in the world and the importance of living life to the fullest. May your journeys be filled with wonder and discovery.

And most especially, to my mom, whose memory lives on in my heart. Your boundless love and unwavering support continue to inspire me every day. This book is for you, **Mom**.

By El Proen

Introduction

Escape the 9-to-5 and Live Your Dreams.

Imagine this: instead of commuting to a stuffy office, you sip coffee on a beach in Bali while tackling your workday. Or perhaps you work from a cozy café in Budapest, exploring the vibrant city during your lunch break. This isn't a fantasy — it's the reality for a growing number of people who have embraced the digital nomad lifestyle.

Fueled by advancements in technology and the increasing acceptance of remote work, the number of digital nomads has skyrocketed in recent years. A staggering recent study by Upwork suggests over 11 million Americans hold remote jobs, and a significant portion of this workforce choose a location-independent lifestyle.

But what exactly is a digital nomad? In essence, digital nomads are professionals who leverage technology to perform their jobs remotely, allowing them to work from anywhere in the world with an internet connection. This opens up a world of possibilities, from exploring new cultures to crafting a work schedule that fits your lifestyle.

The allure of digital nomad jobs extends far beyond exotic locations. Remote work offers a multitude of benefits that traditional office jobs often lack. Imagine ditching the daily commute and enjoying the freedom to work from anywhere. Imagine a flexible schedule that allows you to pursue hobbies, travel, or simply enjoy a healthy work-life balance. These are just some of the advantages that digital nomad careers offer.

This book will be your comprehensive guide to navigating the exciting world of digital nomad jobs. We'll delve into the diverse career options available, equip you with the tools and strategies to land your dream remote position, and guide you through the practicalities of thriving as a digital nomad.

Are you ready to ditch the cubicle and embrace the freedom of the digital nomad lifestyle? Let's get started!

Chapter 1: Demystifying Digital Nomad Jobs

The term "digital nomad job" ignites wanderlust, conjuring up images of working on a laptop with a turquoise ocean view as your backdrop. While that dream can certainly become a reality, the digital nomad landscape extends far beyond idyllic beaches. This chapter delves into the exciting and diverse world of remote work opportunities that allow you to ditch the cubicle and embrace a location-independent career.

A World of Remote Work Possibilities

Digital nomad jobs encompass a vast array of professions, all united by the common thread of being performed remotely with a reliable internet connection. This flexibility opens doors to a multitude of career paths, catering to a wide range of skillsets and interests. Here are just a few examples to spark your imagination:

- **Content Creation:** Are you a wordsmith with a knack for storytelling? Do you have a keen eye for design or a passion for capturing captivating visuals? Content creators are in high demand in the digital nomad sphere. Writers, editors, videographers, graphic designers, and social media managers can thrive in this realm, crafting engaging content for websites, blogs, social media platforms, and marketing campaigns.

- **Marketing Mavens:** The digital marketing landscape offers a plethora of remote work opportunities for skilled individuals. Specialize in areas like Search Engine Optimization (SEO), email marketing, social media marketing, or content marketing, helping businesses from across the globe reach their target audience and achieve their marketing goals.

- **Web Development Wizards:** If you possess the technical prowess of a web developer, the world is your remote oyster! Find freelance gigs or secure remote positions with companies, building and maintaining websites and applications that power businesses and organizations.

- **Customer Service Champions:** The rise of e-commerce and online interactions has fueled the demand for remote customer service professionals. Provide exceptional customer support from anywhere in the world, assisting clients with inquiries, troubleshooting issues, and ensuring a positive customer experience.

- **Virtual Assistant Extraordinaire:** Digital nomads can leverage their diverse skillsets to provide administrative, technical, or creative assistance to clients remotely. Virtual assistants handle a wide range of tasks, from scheduling appointments and managing emails to data entry and social media management.

- **The Limitless Landscape:** The possibilities for remote work are truly boundless! From programmers and accountants to translators and educators, a multitude of professions can be adapted to a digital nomad lifestyle. Do you have a unique skill or passion? With creativity and resourcefulness, you can likely find a way to turn it into a thriving remote career.

Essential Skills for the Digital Nomad Toolkit

Beyond specific job titles and technical expertise, there are core skills that employers actively seek in remote workers:

Communication Powerhouse: The ability to articulate ideas clearly, both verbally and in writing, is paramount for remote collaboration. Express yourself effectively, actively listen to understand client needs, and ensure seamless communication across different time zones and cultures.

Time Management Maestro: Waving goodbye to the traditional office environment doesn't mean waving goodbye to structure. Remote work requires self-discipline and exceptional time management skills. Develop effective strategies to stay focused, prioritize tasks, and meet deadlines consistently, even without the physical presence of a supervisor.

Tech-Savvy Master: Familiarity with project management tools, communication platforms, and relevant software for your chosen field is a must. From cloud-based storage solutions and collaboration tools to industry-specific software programs, equip yourself with the technological know-how to excel in your remote role.

Problem-Solving Sherlock: The ability to identify and solve problems independently is crucial for remote work. You may not always have immediate access to colleagues for assistance. Develop your critical thinking skills, research effectively, and be resourceful to overcome challenges and deliver results.

Adaptability Ace: The digital nomad lifestyle thrives on flexibility and the ability to adjust to new environments and work styles. Embrace the ever-changing scenery, embrace new cultures, and be willing to adapt your routine or workflow as needed to maintain productivity and thrive in different locations.

Debunking the Myths: Unpacking the Realities of Digital Nomad Life

The digital nomad lifestyle is often romanticized, portrayed as an endless vacation with a constant stream of income. While it offers incredible flexibility and the opportunity to travel the world, it's important to address some common misconceptions:

Myth #1: Easy Money Machine: Building a successful digital nomad career requires hard work, dedication, and a continuous commitment to honing your skills and staying relevant in your field. While income potential can be high, unrealistic expectations about instant wealth can lead to disappointment. Be prepared to invest time and effort into establishing yourself and building a strong client base.

Myth #2: Non-Stop Travel Frenzy: While travel is a major perk of the digital nomad lifestyle, it's not always about constantly being on the move. Many digital nomads establish a home base for extended periods to maintain focus, manage work logistics, and create a sense of routine. This allows them to build a local community, explore a particular region in depth, and avoid the constant unpacking and re-packing that comes with perpetual travel.

- **Myth #3: Isolation Nation:** The misconception of digital nomads being lonely souls working in remote corners of the world is fading fast. The digital nomad community thrives online and flourishes in co-working spaces around the globe. Through online forums, social media groups, and co-working communities, you can connect with like-minded individuals, share experiences, build friendships, and find a strong support network on the road.

Beyond the Basics: Building a Fulfilling Digital Nomad Career

This chapter has provided a foundational understanding of the diverse remote work opportunities and essential skills for digital nomads. However, embarking on this exciting career path requires more than just a laptop and a Wi-Fi connection. In the following chapters, we'll delve deeper into:

- **Identifying Your Ideal Digital Nomad Career:** Explore personality and skills assessments, uncover in-depth analyses of popular digital nomad job categories, and discover resources to develop the necessary skills for your chosen path.
- **Building Your Remote-Ready Resume and Cover Letter:** Learn how to craft compelling remote work resumes that showcase your skills and experience, and master the art of writing cover letters that resonate with potential employers in a remote setting.
- **Mastering the Art of the Remote Job Interview:** We'll equip you with strategies to ace remote job interviews, address common interview red flags specific to digital nomad positions, and provide guidance on tackling behavioral interview questions effectively in a virtual setting.

By delving into these crucial aspects and incorporating the valuable insights from experienced digital nomads, you'll be well on your way to building a fulfilling and successful remote career that allows you to travel the world and live life on your own terms.

Chapter 2: Identifying Your Ideal Digital Nomad Career: Charting Your Course to Remote Work Freedom

Land Your Dream Remote Job: The Ultimate Guide to Digital Nomad Careers

The allure of the digital nomad lifestyle lies in the freedom to choose your work, your location, and your way of life. But before you pack your bags and set off to explore the world as a remote worker, it's crucial to embark on a journey of self-discovery. This chapter equips you with the tools and strategies to identify your ideal digital nomad career, ensuring your remote work path aligns with your skills, passions, and lifestyle aspirations.

Finding Your Perfect Fit: A Journey of Self-Awareness

Launching a successful digital nomad career requires introspection and a clear understanding of your strengths, interests, and desired work environment. Don't rush into job applications; instead, invest time in self-assessment to ensure you're setting yourself up for success. Here are some exercises to guide you on this journey:

Skills Inventory: Create a comprehensive list of your existing skills, both technical and soft skills. This includes your past work experience, any relevant certifications you hold, and even transferable skills from hobbies or volunteer work. Be honest and realistic about your skill level in each area.

Passion Project: We all have areas of genuine interest and hidden talents. Identify your passions – what are you naturally drawn to? Could you translate those passions into a viable remote career path? For instance, a love for travel photography could lead to a career in travel blogging or social media management for tourism companies.

Workstyle Preferences: Understanding your ideal work environment is crucial for long-term satisfaction. Do you thrive in a collaborative atmosphere with regular interaction with colleagues, or do you prefer the autonomy of independent work? Consider your preferred work schedule – do you function best with a set structure or relish the flexibility of flexible hours?

Lifestyle Goals: The digital nomad lifestyle isn't a one-size-fits-all solution. Envision the kind of life you want to create for yourself. Consider factors like your desired income level, how often you plan to travel, and the type of locations you'd like to work from. Do you crave bustling cityscapes or peaceful beachside retreats?

Exploring High-Demand Digital Nomad Job Categories

Having a better understanding of yourself provides a solid foundation for exploring the exciting realm of digital nomad careers. Here are some popular and in-demand job categories that offer remote work opportunities:

By El Proen

- **Content Creation:** Are you a wordsmith with a knack for storytelling? Do you possess a keen eye for design or a passion for capturing captivating visuals? The content creation industry offers a plethora of remote work options. Writers, editors, videographers, graphic designers, and social media managers are all in high demand to create engaging content for websites, blogs, social media platforms, and marketing campaigns.

- **Marketing Mavens:** The digital marketing landscape is a haven for skilled and creative individuals seeking remote work opportunities. If you have a passion for branding, a strategic mind, and a knack for online marketing, you can specialize in areas like Search Engine Optimization (SEO), email marketing, social media marketing, or content marketing, helping businesses from across the globe reach their target audience and achieve their marketing goals.

- **Web Development Wizards:** If you possess the technical prowess of a web developer, the world is your remote oyster! Find freelance gigs or secure remote positions with companies, building and maintaining websites and applications that power businesses and organizations. Your skills are valuable assets in the digital nomad world.

- **Customer Service Champions:** The rise of e-commerce and online interactions has fueled the demand for remote customer service professionals. If you have excellent communication skills, a patient demeanor, and a desire to help others, you can provide exceptional customer support from anywhere in the world, assisting clients with inquiries, troubleshooting issues, and ensuring a positive customer experience.

- **Virtual Assistant Extraordinaire:** Digital nomads can leverage their diverse skillsets to provide administrative, technical, or creative assistance to clients remotely. Virtual assistants handle a wide range of tasks, from scheduling appointments and managing emails to data entry and social media management. This is a flexible and adaptable career path that allows you to work with a variety of clients.

Narrowing Your Focus: Honing Your Competitive Edge

By analyzing your skills, interests, and preferences alongside the available job categories, you can start narrowing your focus on the digital nomad career path that aligns perfectly with you. Here are some additional tips to refine your search and increase your chances of landing your dream remote job:

- **Research Specific Jobs:** Once you've identified a few job categories that pique your interest, delve deeper into specific job titles within those fields. Learn about the required skills and experience for each position, the typical tasks involved, and the salary ranges to set realistic expectations.

Upskilling for Success: Continuous learning is paramount in the ever-evolving digital world. Take online courses, pursue relevant certifications, or attend workshops to enhance your existing skills or acquire new ones in your chosen field. This will make you a more competitive candidate in the job market and open doors to more remote work opportunities.

The Network Effect: The digital nomad community thrives on connection and collaboration. Connect with established digital nomads through online forums, social media groups, or professional networking platforms like LinkedIn. Gain valuable insights from their experiences, learn from their successes and challenges, and build a network of support as you embark on your remote work journey.

Craft a Compelling Online Presence: In the digital nomad world, your online presence is your professional calling card. Develop a professional website or online portfolio showcasing your skills and experience. Be active on relevant social media platforms, engage in industry discussions, and position yourself as a thought leader in your chosen field.

Remember, finding your ideal digital nomad career is a process of self-discovery, exploration, and continuous learning. By investing time in understanding yourself, actively refining your skillset, and building valuable connections within the remote work community, you'll be well-equipped to navigate the exciting world of digital nomad careers and create a fulfilling work-life experience that allows you to travel the world and live life on your own terms.

Chapter 3: Building Your Remote-Ready Resume and Cover Letter: Keys to Unlocking Your Digital Nomad Career

Your resume and cover letter are the battle cries in your job search, and in the digital nomad landscape, these documents need to be finely tuned to resonate with remote employers. This chapter equips you with the strategies to craft compelling applications that showcase your unique skills and experience, propelling you towards your dream remote position.

Tailoring Your Resume for Remote Work Success

In the traditional job market, resumes often focus on physical presence and in-office achievements. However, for digital nomad careers, the focus shifts to highlighting the skills and experience that empower you to thrive in a remote work environment. Here's how to optimize your resume for remote work:

- **Spotlight Remote Experience:** If you have any prior remote work experience, don't relegate it to the shadows. Prominently display it in your work history section. Emphasize the skills you honed while working remotely, such as self-management, mastering communication via online platforms, and consistently meeting deadlines independently.

- **Quantify Your Achievements:** Numbers speak volumes. Use data and metrics to showcase the impact of your work. Did you manage a remote team and achieve significant results? Did you increase website traffic by a noteworthy percentage while working remotely? Quantify your contributions to grab the employer's attention and demonstrate your value.

- **Relevant Skills Take Center Stage:** Carefully review the job description and tailor your resume keywords accordingly. Highlight skills like communication, time management, and project management that are essential for remote success. Showcase your proficiency in using project management tools and communication platforms relevant to the job you're applying for.

- **Applicant Tracking Systems (ATS) Savvy:** Many companies use ATS to scan resumes for relevant keywords. While incorporating relevant keywords is crucial, avoid keyword stuffing that can appear unnatural and hinder your application. Find a balance between including the necessary keywords and maintaining a clear, concise, and readable resume.

Crafting a Compelling Cover Letter: Your Remote Work Pitch

Your cover letter is your opportunity to shine beyond the bullet points of your resume. It's your chance to tell a compelling story, showcase your personality, and convince the hiring manager that you're the perfect fit for the remote position. Here are some key strategies to craft a winning cover letter for a digital nomad job:

- **Personalization is Key:** Address the hiring manager by name whenever possible. This demonstrates effort and genuine interest in the specific opportunity. Briefly mention where you found the job posting and express your enthusiasm for the position and the company.

- **Highlight Your Remote Fit:** Don't wait until the later stages of your cover letter to address your suitability for a remote role. Early on, emphasize your ability to thrive in a remote work environment. Mention your experience working remotely or your strong organizational and time management skills that make you a prime candidate for a remote position.

Showcase Your Skills and Experience in Action: Don't just list the skills and experiences mentioned in your resume. Briefly elaborate on relevant skills and experiences, but do so with a specific focus on the job requirements. Provide concrete examples of how you've leveraged these skills to achieve success in previous roles, especially in remote work settings.

Quantify Your Accomplishments: Similar to your resume, use data and metrics to demonstrate the value you can bring to the company. Highlight achievements that showcase your ability to deliver results in a remote setting. Quantifiable examples add credibility and give the hiring manager a clearer picture of your impact.

Express Your Passion (and Wanderlust): Conclude by reiterating your enthusiasm for the opportunity and the company. Briefly mention your excitement about the potential to work remotely as a digital nomad. Express your passion for the role and how it aligns with your desire to travel and explore (while still delivering exceptional results).

Cover Letter Example for a Digital Nomad Job (Revised)

Dear [Hiring Manager name],

I am writing with fervent enthusiasm to express my keen interest in the [Job title] position advertised on [Platform where you found the job]. As a highly motivated and results-oriented [Your profession] with [Number] years of experience, I possess the skillset and experience necessary to excel in this role, particularly within a remote work environment.

Throughout my career, I have a proven track record of [List relevant achievements related to the job description]. In my previous role at [Previous company], I successfully [Describe a specific achievement that showcases a remote-friendly skill, e.g., managed a virtual team of 5 content creators and increased website traffic by 20% while working remotely]. My adept communication and time management skills, coupled with my ability to work independently and consistently deliver high-quality results in a remote setting, make me a perfect fit for this position.

As a passionate digital nomad with a yearning to [Mention your reason for pursuing a remote nomad job, e.g., explore the rich tapestry of cultures and immerse myself in new environments while working], I am confident that I can thrive in a remote work environment and contribute significantly to the team's success. My ability to adapt, my commitment to continuous learning, and my enthusiasm for [Mention something specific about the company or industry] make me a valuable asset to your team.

I have attached my resume for your review and would welcome the opportunity to discuss my qualifications further in an interview. Thank you for your time and consideration.

Sincerely,

[Your Name]

Remember, your resume and cover letter are your digital handshake with a potential employer. By tailoring these documents to highlight your remote-work readiness, using strong examples, and conveying your passion for the position, you can increase your chances of landing your dream digital nomad job and embarking on a fulfilling journey of work and exploration.

Chapter 4: Mastering the Art of the Remote Job Interview: Shining on Your Virtual Stage

The remote job interview is your chance to make a stellar first impression and secure your dream digital nomad position. While the core interview principles remain similar to traditional face-to-face encounters, the virtual setting presents unique opportunities and challenges. This chapter equips you with the strategies and know-how to shine brightly on your virtual stage, showcasing your qualifications and landing the remote job that fuels your wanderlust.

Tech Check: Ensuring a Flawless Virtual Performance

Technical preparedness is paramount for a successful remote interview. Here's how to ensure your technology woes don't overshadow your brilliance:

- **Conquer Your Connection:** The internet is your lifeline in a remote interview. Before the interview day arrives, conduct a thorough internet speed test and ensure your connection is stable and reliable. If possible, consider a wired ethernet connection for maximum stability over Wi-Fi.

- **Practice Makes Perfect:** Don't wait until the interview to familiarize yourself with the video conferencing platform being used. Conduct a test run beforehand, ensuring your audio and video are functioning properly, and practice navigating the platform's features.

Light Up Your Professionalism: Find a well-lit location for your interview. Natural light is ideal, but avoid sitting with harsh light directly behind you. If using artificial lighting, opt for soft, diffused light to avoid creating unflattering shadows.

Background Matters: Your virtual background serves as your set design. Choose a clean, professional background free from clutter or distracting elements. A simple, solid-colored wall is a safe choice, or consider using a virtual background provided by the platform if available.

Dress for Success (Remotely): While a suit and tie might not be necessary, dressing professionally for your remote interview projects confidence and establishes a positive first impression. Dress in attire that aligns with the company culture you're interviewing with, while maintaining comfort for a potentially long interview session.

Remote Rockstar: Mastering Video Conferencing Etiquette

The world of video conferencing comes with its own set of etiquette. By following these guidelines, you'll project professionalism and ensure clear communication throughout the interview:

Eye Contact is Key: Maintain eye contact by looking directly into the camera lens during the interview. This creates a sense of attentiveness and engagement, even though you're not making direct eye contact with the interviewer on their screen.

Body Language Matters: Project confidence through your body language. Sit up straight with good posture, and avoid fidgeting or slouching in your chair. Non-verbal cues speak volumes, so ensure yours convey professionalism and enthusiasm.

Mute Yourself When Not Speaking: Minimize background noise by muting your microphone whenever you're not actively speaking. This eliminates any distracting background noises like typing, coughing, or environmental sounds, ensuring clear communication.

Optional: The Power of a Professional Virtual Background: If your physical background isn't ideal or lacks a professional atmosphere, consider using a virtual background provided by the video conferencing platform. This can help create a more polished and professional online presence.

Highlighting Your Remote-Ready Skillset

Throughout the interview, don't just answer questions – weave a captivating narrative that showcases your suitability for a remote work environment. Here are some key skills to emphasize:

- **Work Ethic Champion:** Demonstrate your ability to manage your time effectively, prioritize tasks independently, and consistently meet deadlines without the physical presence of a supervisor. Highlight specific strategies you use to stay focused and productive in a remote setting.
- **Communication Powerhouse:** Strong communication skills are crucial for success in any role, and even more so in a remote environment. Express yourself clearly and concisely, both verbally and in writing. Highlight your ability to actively listen, articulate ideas effectively, and collaborate seamlessly with colleagues online.
- **Adaptability Ace:** The digital nomad lifestyle thrives on flexibility. Convey your ability to adapt to new environments, work styles, and time zones. Mention your experience working remotely (if applicable) or your willingness to learn and adjust to the remote work culture of the company.
- **Problem-Solving Sherlock:** Showcase your ability to identify and solve problems independently. Provide examples from previous work experiences where you tackled challenges remotely and achieved successful outcomes. This demonstrates your resourcefulness and initiative, valuable assets in a remote work setting.

Common Digital Nomad Interview Questions: Acing the Remote Interview Script

By preparing for these commonly asked digital nomad interview questions and practicing your responses, you can confidently showcase your strengths and increase your chances of landing the job:

- **How do you stay motivated and focused while working remotely?** (Discuss your time management strategies, self-discipline techniques, and use of productivity tools.)
- **How do you manage your time effectively in a remote work environment?** (Explain your process for prioritizing tasks, creating a daily schedule, and using project management tools to stay organized.)
- **What strategies do you use to stay connected with colleagues and collaborate remotely?** (Highlight your experience using online communication tools, scheduling regular virtual meetings, and fostering a collaborative online work environment.)

By El Proen

How do you plan to maintain a healthy work-life balance as a digital nomad? (Discuss your strategies for setting boundaries, scheduling breaks, and disconnecting from work during off-work hours to avoid burnout.)

Do you have experience working remotely in different time zones? (If you have experience, provide specific examples. If not, emphasize your willingness to adapt and your research on communication strategies across time zones.)

By preparing thoughtful answers to these questions and incorporating the tips throughout this chapter, you'll be well-equipped to shine in your remote job interview and take a significant step towards launching your fulfilling digital nomad career.

Do not forget, a successful remote job interview is about showcasing your skills, experience, and enthusiasm for remote work. By preparing the technical aspects, mastering video conferencing etiquette, highlighting your remote-ready strengths, and practicing your responses to common interview questions, you'll transform yourself into a confident and compelling candidate, ready to impress and land your dream remote position.

Chapter 5: Unveiling the Treasure Trove: Top Platforms and Resources for Finding Digital Nomad Jobs

The digital nomad lifestyle hinges on the freedom to choose your work and your location. But unearthing your ideal remote position requires venturing beyond the familiar territory of traditional job boards. This chapter equips you with a diverse arsenal of resources, transforming your job search into a successful treasure hunt for the perfect remote work opportunity.

Popular Platforms: Charting Your Course on Remote Job Boards and Communities

The digital nomad job market thrives in a vibrant ecosystem beyond the walls of traditional job boards. Here are some valuable online communities and platforms specifically designed to connect remote workers with exciting opportunities:

Remote.co: Imagine a job board dedicated solely to remote work – that's the magic of Remote.co. Explore a curated selection of remote positions across various industries, all waiting to be discovered by ambitious digital nomads like yourself.

We Work Remotely: Another gem in the remote work landscape, We Work Remotely offers a treasure trove of job listings spanning a wide range of industries. From marketing and design to development and customer service, you're sure to find opportunities that ignite your passions.

- **FlexJobs:** If flexibility is your mantra, FlexJobs is your haven. This platform meticulously curates remote and flexible work opportunities, ensuring you can find a position that aligns perfectly with your digital nomad aspirations.
- **Digital Nomad Soul:** Community isn't just a word; it's the lifeblood of the digital nomad lifestyle. Digital Nomad Soul fosters a vibrant online community where you can connect with fellow nomads, discover job openings, find co-working spaces, and access valuable travel resources – all in one place.
- **Nomad List:** Think of Nomad List as your one-stop shop for all things digital nomad. This comprehensive platform offers a thriving online forum where you can connect and exchange experiences with other nomads. Additionally, explore curated job listings and in-depth location guides to plan your remote work adventures.

Mastering the Art of the Application: Crafting Your Remote Work Narrative

Landing your dream remote job requires more than just submitting a resume. Here's how to transform your application into a compelling narrative that showcases your unique value proposition:

- **Keyword Alchemy:** The art of the job search often involves a touch of magic. Carefully study job descriptions and strategically incorporate relevant keywords throughout your resume and cover letter. This optimization increases your chances of getting noticed by Applicant Tracking Systems (ATS) used by many companies, propelling your application to the top of the pile.
- **Compelling Applications: Beyond the Generic:** Generic applications are a dime a dozen. Craft a personalized cover letter for each position you apply for. Highlight your skills and experience relevant to the specific job, showcasing how you can make a significant contribution to the company. Don't shy away from mentioning your digital nomad lifestyle – briefly explain how your remote work approach aligns perfectly with the opportunity.
- **Freelance Platforms: Stepping Stones to Success:** Freelance platforms like Upwork, Fiverr, or Freelancer.com can be launchpads for your digital nomad career. Explore project-based remote work opportunities to gain valuable experience, build your portfolio, and establish yourself as a skilled remote worker.

Building Your Network: Expanding Your Remote Work Horizons

The digital nomad world thrives on connection. By actively building your network, you unlock a treasure trove of potential opportunities and invaluable insights. Here are some strategies to expand your network and connect with the remote work community:

Online Communities: A Haven for Connection: Join online communities and forums dedicated to digital nomads. Connect with other remote workers, share experiences, learn from each other's journeys, and discover potential job openings through word-of-mouth connections.

Social Media Groups: The Power of Community: The power of social media extends far beyond the realm of cat videos. There are numerous Facebook groups and other social media communities specifically focused on digital nomads and remote work. Utilize these platforms to connect with potential employers, fellow nomads, and industry professionals who can offer valuable guidance and support.

Attend Events: Learning and Networking On (and Offline): If possible, attend online or in-person conferences and events related to remote work and digital nomadism. These events provide excellent opportunities to network with professionals in your field, learn about new job openings, and gain valuable insights from industry leaders.

By leveraging these resources and actively building your network, you'll transform your job search from a solitary pursuit into a collaborative adventure. With dedication, perseverance, and a bit of digital nomad ingenuity, you'll unearth the perfect remote work opportunity that fuels your passions and allows you to explore the world while earning a living.

Chapter 6: Setting Up Your Remote Workspace and Tools: Your Digital Nomad Command Center

As a digital nomad, your workspace is your mission control. Whether you're nestled in a bustling Bangkok coffee shop or a quiet Airbnb in Berlin, crafting a productive and comfortable environment is essential for remote work success. This chapter equips you with the knowledge to transform any space into your personal hub of accomplishment.

Designing Your Ideal Workspace: Location, Comfort, and Inspiration

The perfect remote workspace isn't a one-size-fits-all proposition. Here are some key considerations to shape your ideal work environment:

Land Your Dream Remote Job: The Ultimate Guide to Digital Nomad Careers

- **Location, Location, Location:** Just like real estate, your workspace location matters. Consider factors like noise level, access to natural light, and proximity to essential amenities like coffee shops or co-working spaces. Co-working spaces offer dedicated desks, a sense of community, and a professional atmosphere, while cafes or home offices can provide a more casual vibe. Choose a location that suits your work style and personal preferences.
- **Ergonomics Matter:** Investing in a comfortable chair with good lumbar support is crucial for preventing aches and strains. Ideally, your workspace should promote good posture with your monitor at eye level and your keyboard within easy reach. Don't underestimate the power of ergonomics – a comfortable workspace can significantly enhance your productivity and well-being.
- **Tech Essentials:** Reliable internet connectivity is the lifeblood of remote work. Ensure your chosen workspace offers a stable and strong internet connection to avoid frustrating lags or dropped connections. A good quality laptop is your primary tool, but consider a secondary monitor for increased productivity, especially if you work with multiple programs or documents simultaneously.
- **Personalize Your Space:** Surround yourself with elements that inspire you and promote focus. Family photos, inspiring artwork, or even a potted plant can transform your workspace from functional to motivational. A touch of personalization can significantly enhance your work environment and spark creativity.

Essential Tools for the Remote Work Warrior

Your digital nomad toolkit should be stocked with powerful software and apps to streamline your workflow, keep you organized, and facilitate seamless communication with colleagues and clients:

- **Project Management Mavens:** Project management tools like Asana, Trello, or Basecamp are your secret weapons for staying organized. These applications help you create tasks, assign deadlines, collaborate with team members, and track project progress, ensuring everything stays on track, even when you're halfway across the world.
- **Communication Champions:** Stay connected and engaged with your team using video conferencing platforms like Zoom, Google Meet, or Skype. Schedule regular video calls to discuss projects, brainstorm ideas, and maintain a sense of connection with colleagues,

even in a remote setting. Additionally, instant messaging apps like Slack can facilitate quick communication and team discussions, keeping everyone in the loop.

Cloud Storage Crusaders: Cloud storage services like Dropbox, Google Drive, or Microsoft OneDrive are your digital safety nets. Store your files securely in the cloud, ensuring accessibility from any device, anywhere in the world. Cloud storage provides peace of mind, knowing your important documents are always within reach, no matter your location.

Productivity Powerhouses: Utilize time management apps like RescueTime or Focus Keeper to stay focused and on track with your deadlines. These applications can help you track your time spent on different tasks, identify areas for improvement, and maintain a productive work rhythm. Password managers like LastPass can securely store your login credentials, eliminating the frustration of forgotten passwords.

Staying Organized and Mastering Your Workload

Conquering your workload as a digital nomad requires effective organization and a strategic approach to managing your time. Here are some key strategies to cultivate a productive and sustainable remote work routine:

Craft a Daily Schedule: Establish a routine that incorporates focused work time, dedicated breaks, and time for self-care. Schedule your most important tasks for your peak productivity hours, and allocate time for emails, administrative tasks, and breaks throughout the day. Having a clear schedule helps you prioritize tasks and avoid feeling overwhelmed.

Prioritization is Key: Use to-do lists and prioritize your tasks based on urgency and importance. Tackle the most important tasks first and break down larger projects into smaller, manageable steps. Prioritization keeps you focused on what matters most and ensures you meet deadlines efficiently.

Calendars and Reminders: Your Digital Timekeepers: Set reminders for deadlines, appointments, and important meetings using online calendars like Google Calendar or Apple Calendar. These tools help you stay on top of your schedule and avoid missed deadlines.

Batch Similar Tasks Together: Group similar tasks together to improve efficiency and minimize context switching. For example, dedicate a specific time block to responding to emails or scheduling calls. Batching tasks reduces the time spent mentally transitioning between different activities.

- **The Art of Delegation: Empowering Others for Shared Success (if applicable)**
For digital nomads managing freelance projects or virtual teams, delegation becomes a powerful tool for maximizing productivity and achieving your goals. Here's how to effectively delegate tasks while maintaining control and ensuring quality outcomes:

- **Identify Tasks Suitable for Delegation:** Not all tasks are created equal. Analyze your workload and identify repetitive, administrative, or skill-specific tasks that can be effectively delegated to capable team members or freelancers. Focus on delegating tasks that free up your time for core responsibilities that require your unique expertise.

- **Choose the Right Person for the Job:** Matching tasks to the right skillset is crucial for successful delegation. Consider the strengths and experience of your team members or potential freelancers when assigning tasks. Delegate tasks to individuals who possess the necessary skills and experience to complete them effectively.

- **Provide Clear Instructions and Expectations:** Don't set your team or freelancers up for failure. Clearly communicate the task at hand, including the desired outcome, deadlines, and any specific instructions or protocols to be followed. Providing clear expectations ensures everyone is on the same page and minimizes the risk of misunderstandings.

- **Empowerment Through Resources and Support:** Set your team or freelancers up for success by providing them with the necessary resources and support. This might include access to relevant documents, training materials, or collaboration tools. Empowering your team fosters a sense of ownership and increases the likelihood of successful task completion.

- **Open Communication and Feedback Loops:** Delegation doesn't mean relinquishing all control. Maintain open communication channels with your team or freelancers. Schedule regular check-ins to discuss progress, address any questions or concerns, and offer constructive feedback. Open communication builds trust and ensures tasks stay on track.

- **Recognize and Reward Achievements:** Acknowledging a job well done is a powerful motivator. Recognize and appreciate the contributions of your team or freelancers when they successfully complete delegated tasks. This positive reinforcement encourages continued excellence and strengthens your working relationships.

By effectively delegating tasks, you can free up valuable time to focus on strategic initiatives and core responsibilities, ultimately leading to increased productivity and achieving your business goals. Remember, delegation is not about abdicating responsibility; it's about empowering others and fostering a collaborative work environment where everyone thrives.

Chapter 7: Building a Sustainable Digital Nomad Lifestyle: Work, Wellness, and Wanderlust in Perfect Harmony

The digital nomad lifestyle isn't just a glamorous Instagram feed; it's about crafting a holistic and sustainable way of living that fuels your wanderlust while ensuring financial security, physical well-being, and a strong sense of connection. This chapter equips you with the knowledge and strategies to navigate the financial realities of remote work, prioritize your health on the road, and build a supportive network wherever your travels take you.

Financial Freedom: Budgeting for Adventure Without Breaking the Bank

Budgeting Bonanza: Creating a realistic budget is the cornerstone of financial freedom as a digital nomad. Factor in your income streams, travel costs, accommodation expenses (considering everything from hostels to house-sitting gigs), and living expenses (which can vary greatly depending on your location). Budgeting apps and spreadsheets can be your secret weapons for tracking income and expenses, ensuring you stay on track financially throughout your journeys.

Cost-Conscious Travel: Stretching Your Dollars Further: Embrace travel strategies that maximize your experiences while minimizing your financial footprint. Consider house-sitting opportunities, volunteering programs that provide accommodation, or budget-friendly travel destinations. Travel hacking with rewards credit cards can also generate additional savings on flights and accommodations.

Taxes on the Go: Staying Compliant, Wherever You Roam: Taxes can be a minefield for digital nomads. Research tax implications for remote workers in different countries, especially if you're working for a company based in your home country. Consulting a tax professional can ensure you're filing correctly and avoiding any unwanted surprises come tax season.

- **Building a Safety Net: Peace of Mind for the Mobile Professional:** Life throws curveballs, and the digital nomad lifestyle is no exception. Consider building an emergency fund to cover unexpected expenses or potential income gaps between projects. A financial safety net provides peace of mind and allows you to focus on exploring the world with confidence.

Healthy Habits for the Remote Worker on the Move

- **Routine is Your Friend:** Maintaining a regular sleep schedule, even with changing time zones, is crucial for your physical and mental well-being. Incorporate physical activity into your daily routine, even while traveling. Pack workout clothes and utilize apps for bodyweight exercises or yoga routines that you can do anywhere, anytime.

- **Nourishing Your Body for Peak Performance:** Eating healthy can be a challenge on the road, but it's essential for maintaining your energy levels and overall health. Plan your meals in advance whenever possible, visit local farmer's markets for fresh produce, and research healthy restaurant options when dining out.

- **Prioritizing Mental Wellness: De-stressing on Demand:** The constant novelty and potential isolation of remote work can be stressful. Practice mindfulness techniques like meditation or deep breathing exercises to manage stress and maintain mental clarity. Consider scheduling virtual therapy sessions or joining online communities for remote workers to connect with others who understand the unique challenges of the digital nomad lifestyle.

Work-Life Balance: Finding Harmony Between Productivity and Exploration

- **Boundaries are Beautiful:** Establishing clear boundaries between work and personal life is essential to avoid burnout. Communicate your working hours clearly with clients and colleagues. Avoid checking work emails or taking calls outside of your designated work hours. Respect your downtime and use it to recharge and explore your surroundings.

- **Embrace the Flexibility:** One of the greatest perks of remote work is flexibility. Take advantage of it! Schedule breaks throughout the day to explore your surroundings, pursue hobbies, or simply relax. The flexibility of the digital nomad lifestyle allows you to design a work schedule that aligns with your travel itinerary and personal interests.

- **Disconnect to Reconnect:** Technology is a powerful tool, but it can also be a distraction. Schedule regular digital detox periods to disconnect from your devices and truly immerse yourself in the present moment. Unplug, explore new places, and use your free time to recharge and reconnect with yourself and the world around you.

Building Your Digital Nomad Network: Cultivating Connections in a World of Constant Change

The Power of Online Communities: The digital nomad world thrives on connection. Stay connected with fellow remote workers through online forums, social media groups dedicated to digital nomads, and co-working spaces. These online communities provide a platform to share experiences, offer support, find travel buddies or collaborators, and build a sense of belonging, even when you're miles away from home.

Local is the New Global: Expanding Your Horizons Beyond the Digital World: While online connections are valuable, don't underestimate the power of in-person interaction. Participate in local events, volunteer in your temporary communities, and join co-working spaces to connect with people beyond the digital realm. Immersing yourself in the local culture is a rewarding experience that expands your horizons and fosters a deeper connection to the places you visit.

Embrace the Cultural Tapestry: Building Bridges Through Understanding: Learning a few basic phrases in the local language can go a long way in establishing rapport with locals. Show genuine interest in the cultures you encounter, try new foods with an open mind, and be open to new experiences. Embracing cultural differences fosters meaningful connections and enriches your digital nomad journey.

By cultivating financial responsibility, prioritizing your health and well-being, and actively building a supportive network of connections, you can transform the digital nomad lifestyle from a dream into a sustainable reality. This approach allows you to experience the world on your own terms, work remotely with purpose, and create a life filled with adventure, fulfillment, and meaningful connections.

Chapter 8: Essential Resources and Tools for Digital Nomads: Your Nomadic Toolkit for Success

The digital nomad lifestyle offers unparalleled freedom and flexibility, but navigating the logistical realities requires a well-equipped toolkit. This chapter equips you with the essential resources and tools to streamline your nomadic adventures, from finding suitable accommodation and planning your travels to managing your work-life balance and staying informed about legalities.

Finding Your Home Away From Home: Accommodations for the Modern Nomad

- **Accommodation Platforms: A World of Options:** Platforms like Airbnb, Nomad List Rentals, and Trusted Housesitters offer a vast selection of accommodation options tailored to the digital nomad lifestyle. Explore apartments, shared living spaces, unique guesthouses, or even house-sitting opportunities to find the perfect home base for your remote work adventures.

- **Co-living Communities: Fostering Connection and Collaboration:** Consider co-living spaces designed specifically for remote workers. These communities offer private rooms or shared accommodations, along with dedicated co-working areas, social events, and opportunities to connect with fellow nomads, fostering a sense of belonging and collaboration.

- **Digital Nomad Hubs: Thriving Ecosystems for Remote Work:** Research popular digital nomad destinations known for established remote work communities and infrastructure. These locations often boast co-working spaces, reliable and affordable internet access, and visa options suitable for extended stays, allowing you to seamlessly blend work and travel.

Planning Your Nomadic Adventures: Charting Your Course Across the Globe

- **Travel Planning Powerhouses:** Leverage travel planning websites like Skyscanner, Kayak, or Google Flights to find the most affordable flights and accommodation deals for your nomadic adventures. Consider travel insurance specifically designed for digital nomads to provide peace of mind and protection against unexpected events.

- **Visa Savvy: Understanding the Rules of the Road:** Research visa options for the countries you plan to visit and work remotely from. Websites like Nomad List and VisaGuide.World are valuable resources, providing comprehensive information on visa requirements for remote workers in various locations. Remember, visa regulations can change, so staying updated is crucial.

- **Nomad Travel Blogs and Guides: Insights from the Road Less Traveled:** Numerous travel blogs and guidebooks cater specifically to the digital nomad community. These resources offer invaluable insights into the cost of living, internet connectivity, visa information, must-see attractions, and hidden gems in various locations, empowering you to make informed decisions about your nomadic journey.

Work-Life Balance for Nomads: Staying Productive and Thriving on the Move

Time Management Masters: Apps to Keep You on Track: Utilize time tracking and project management apps like RescueTime, Toggl Track, or Asana to stay organized and manage your workload efficiently while traveling. These tools help you prioritize tasks, track your billable hours, and meet deadlines, even when your work environment is constantly changing.

Productivity on the Go: Minimizing Distractions and Maximizing Focus: Explore apps like Freedom or Focus Keeper that help you minimize distractions and maintain focus during work hours, even in unfamiliar environments. These productivity boosters can significantly enhance your ability to get things done, no matter where your travels take you.

Wellness Apps: Maintaining Your Well-being on the Road: Consider incorporating meditation apps like Headspace or Calm into your routine to manage stress and promote relaxation while traveling. Fitness apps like Nike Training Club or YogaGlo offer convenient workout routines you can do anywhere, ensuring you stay active and maintain a healthy lifestyle throughout your nomadic adventures.

Staying Informed and Connected: Building Your Remote Work Network

Digital Nomad Communities: A Wealth of Shared Experiences: Join online communities like Digital Nomad Soul, Nomad List Forums, or The Remote Work Tribe. These platforms connect digital nomads from all over the world, allowing you to share experiences, ask questions, find valuable resources, and gain insights from fellow remote workers who understand the unique challenges and rewards of the nomadic lifestyle.

Social Media Groups: Expanding Your Network and Staying Updated: There are numerous Facebook Groups and other social media communities dedicated to digital nomads and remote work. Utilize these platforms to connect with potential employers, network with fellow nomads, stay updated on industry trends and job opportunities, and build a strong support network on your nomadic journey.

Legal and Tax Resources: Navigating the Rules of Remote Work: Consult websites or legal professionals specializing in remote work regulations. Stay informed about tax implications for digital nomads, especially when working for companies based in your home country. Understanding legal and tax requirements is essential for ensuring a smooth and compliant nomadic experience.

By leveraging these essential resources and tools, you can streamline your digital nomad lifestyle, navigate logistical challenges with confidence, and stay connected to the vibrant remote work community. Remember, information can change, so ongoing research and staying updated on legalities are essential for a successful and fulfilling nomadic experience. This well-equipped toolkit empowers you to embrace the freedom and flexibility of the digital nomad lifestyle while staying organized, productive, and informed throughout your global adventures.

Chapter 9: Digital Nomadism Across Life Stages: Charting Your Course for a Fulfilling Journey

The digital nomad lifestyle offers unparalleled freedom and flexibility, but it's important to acknowledge that it's not a monolithic experience. This chapter explores the challenges and considerations faced by digital nomads at different life stages, equipping you with practical advice for navigating these situations and crafting a fulfilling nomadic journey.

Traveling with Children: Balancing Adventure and Family Needs

While the digital nomad lifestyle can be an enriching experience for children, it also presents unique challenges:

- **Balancing Work and Childcare:** Ensuring a healthy balance between work commitments and childcare responsibilities can be a constant juggling act. Finding reliable childcare options in new locations can be difficult, and adapting to different educational systems adds another layer of complexity.

Practical Strategies for Nomadic Families:

- **Destination Decisiveness:** Consider destinations with established expat communities or international schools that can provide a sense of stability and continuity for your children's education.
- **Co-working with Care:** Research co-working spaces that offer childcare facilities or explore virtual babysitting services to free up dedicated work time.
- **Schedule Savvy:** Plan your work schedule strategically around nap times and breaks to ensure you can dedicate quality time to your children's needs and development.

Homeschooling on the Go: Embrace homeschooling resources or online learning platforms to maintain educational progress for your children, regardless of your location.

Travel Buddies by Choice: Involve your children in travel planning, allowing them to choose destinations or activities that pique their interests. This fosters a sense of ownership and excitement about your nomadic adventures.

Managing Remote Work While Caring for Elderly Parents

Balancing remote work with the needs of aging parents presents a distinct set of challenges:

Scheduling Conflicts: Scheduling work hours can be challenging when you need to accommodate appointments or emergencies related to your parents' care. Managing potential guilt or emotional stress is also a significant consideration.

Practical Strategies for Remote Caregivers:

Flexible Work Arrangements: Discuss flexible work arrangements with your employer to accommodate unexpected situations or appointments related to your parents' care.

The Power of Technology: Utilize technology like video conferencing to stay connected with your parents and caregivers, providing a sense of security and normalcy.

Delegation for Daily Needs: Consider hiring remote assistants or part-time help to manage errands or light caregiving duties, freeing up your time and energy.

Senior Care Research: Research elder care options in potential travel destinations, particularly if you plan on extended stays in specific locations.

Open Communication is Key: Communicate openly with your parents about your travel plans and involve them in the decision-making process as much as possible. This fosters trust and understanding throughout your nomadic journey.

General Considerations for Digital Nomads Across Life Stages

Financial Foresight: Factor in additional expenses for childcare, healthcare, or elder care when budgeting for your travels. Building a realistic financial plan is essential for a sustainable nomadic lifestyle.

Building Your Support Network: Connect with other digital nomad families online or in co-working spaces. Sharing experiences and advice with those who understand your unique challenges can be invaluable.

By El Proen

- **Embrace the Unexpected:** The beauty of the digital nomad lifestyle lies in its flexibility. Be prepared to adapt your plans or routines as needed, and embrace the unexpected experiences that arise throughout your journeys.

By carefully considering the unique challenges and opportunities presented at different life stages, you can craft a digital nomad experience that is fulfilling for you and your loved ones. Remember, with the right planning, adaptability, and a supportive network, you can navigate the joys and challenges of remote work while living a life filled with adventure, exploration, and meaningful connections.

Chapter 10: The Digital Nomad Entrepreneur: Building Your Remote Business

The digital nomad lifestyle isn't just about remote work; it can also be a launchpad for your entrepreneurial dreams. This chapter provides a roadmap for aspiring digital nomad entrepreneurs, covering the essential steps to starting and running a successful remote business.

Business Planning:

- **Identify Your Niche:** What problem can your business solve? Who is your target audience?
- **Develop a Business Model:** How will you generate revenue? What are your pricing strategies?
- **Craft a Business Plan:** Outline your goals, market research, marketing strategies, financial projections, and operational plan.

Marketing Strategies for Remote Audiences:

- **Build a Strong Online Presence:** Create a professional website, utilize social media effectively, and engage in content marketing to attract potential customers.
- **Leverage Online Marketplaces:** Explore platforms like Upwork, Fiverr, or Freelancer to find clients and showcase your services.
- **Network with Other Remote Businesses:** Connect with other digital nomads and entrepreneurs online or at co-working spaces to build partnerships and expand your reach.
- **Focus on Building Relationships:** Provide excellent customer service and build trust with your clients to foster long-term relationships.

Legal Considerations for International Businesses:

Register Your Business: Research and comply with business registration requirements in your home country and any countries you plan to operate from.

Taxes: Understand your tax obligations in different countries and consult a tax professional to ensure compliance.

Visas and Work Permits: Research visa requirements for remote work in different locations, especially if you plan on extended stays.

Finding Mentors and Resources:

Online Courses and Workshops: Numerous online resources offer guidance on starting and running a remote business.

Remote Business Coaching and Mentorship Programs: Invest in mentorship from experienced remote entrepreneurs for personalized advice and support.

Digital Nomad Communities: Connect with other digital nomad entrepreneurs online or in co-working spaces to share experiences, challenges, and resources.

By taking these steps, you can transform your digital nomad lifestyle into a thriving remote business venture. Remember, success requires dedication, continuous learning, and the ability to adapt to the ever-evolving online landscape.

Chapter 11: The Future of Digital Nomad Work:

Digital nomads with strong analytical skills and the ability to adapt to new technologies will be well-positioned to thrive in the future of remote work.

The Rise of the Gig Economy:

The gig economy, characterized by short-term contracts and freelance work, is likely to continue expanding, offering flexibility for digital nomads.

However, it's crucial to develop strategies for finding consistent work and managing income fluctuations.

The Blurring Lines Between Work and Travel:

As technology facilitates remote work, the lines between work and travel may become increasingly blurred.

Digital nomads will need to develop strong time management skills and establish healthy boundaries to maintain a good work-life balance.

The Importance of Continuous Learning:

- The remote work landscape is dynamic, and staying ahead of the curve will be essential for digital nomads.
- Embracing continuous learning through online courses, workshops, and professional development opportunities will be crucial for success.

The Potential Impact of Geopolitical Events:

- Geopolitical events and economic fluctuations can impact internet access, travel restrictions, and currency exchange rates, affecting digital nomads.
- Staying informed and having a backup plan is vital for navigating these uncertainties.

The Evolution of Coworking Spaces:

- Coworking spaces will likely evolve to cater specifically to the needs of digital nomads, offering amenities like childcare facilities, travel consultations, and language exchange programs.

The Rise of Remote Work Hubs:

- Certain destinations may emerge as remote work hubs, attracting digital nomads with infrastructure, visa options, and vibrant communities specifically designed to cater to their needs.

The Future is Remote:

The future of work is increasingly remote, and digital nomads are at the forefront of this exciting trend. By embracing new technologies, developing adaptability, and continuously learning, digital nomads can thrive in the ever-evolving work landscape.

This chapter on the future of digital nomad work highlights the dynamic nature of this lifestyle. The key to success lies in adaptability, continuous learning, and a willingness to embrace change. With the right approach and a proactive mindset, digital nomads can continue to enjoy the freedom, flexibility, and global opportunities that this unique career path offers.

Conclusion

Escape the Cubicle and Embrace Your Dream Digital Nomad Lifestyle

The digital nomad lifestyle offers a world of possibilities for those seeking a career that blends remote work with adventure. This book has equipped you with the knowledge and resources to navigate this exciting path.

Key Steps to Your Digital Nomad Journey:

Self-Discovery: Identify your strengths, interests, and desired work environment to find your ideal digital nomad career path.

Skill Up: Develop or hone the skills and qualifications sought after by remote employers in your chosen field.

Craft Your Digital Brand: Build a compelling resume and cover letter that highlight your remote-work readiness.

Land Your Dream Job: Utilize the resources provided to find remote work opportunities and ace your remote job interviews.

Thrive as a Digital Nomad: Set up a productive workspace, manage your finances effectively, and prioritize your health and well-being while traveling.

Take Action and Live Your Dreams:

The world is your office with a digital nomad career. Don't let fear or uncertainty hold you back. Take the first step today! Research specific job titles, explore online courses, and start building your remote work portfolio.

Additional Resources and Next Steps:

Downloadable Templates: Access downloadable templates for crafting a resume optimized for remote jobs and writing compelling cover letters that land interviews.

Further Reading: Explore the suggested reading list to delve deeper into specific aspects of digital nomad life, such as travel hacking, remote work productivity, and navigating the financial realities of a location-independent career.

With this in mind, the digital nomad lifestyle is an adventure waiting to unfold. Embrace the flexibility to work from anywhere, the freedom to explore new cultures, and the countless experiences waiting to enrich your life! With the knowledge and resources provided in this book, you can turn your dream of remote work and exploration into reality.

By El Proen

Did you find this book helpful? Your feedback is valuable and helps me create even better resources for aspiring digital nomads. Please consider leaving a review on Amazon to share your thoughts.

By El Proen